I0715578

HUNGER HOUSE

POEMS

HUNGER HOUSE (c) 2025 **Jessica Turcat**
All Rights Reserved

No part of this book may be used or reproduced in any manner whatsoever without permission except in the case of brief quotations embodied in critical essays or reviews.

This is a work of the poet's iumadination. Any references to historical events, real people, or real places are used fictitiously. Other names, characters, places, and events are products of the author's imagination, and any resemblance to actual events or places or persons, living or dead, is entirely coincidental.

Attention schools and businesses; for discounted copies on large orders please contact the publisher directly.

Kallisto Gaia Press Inc.
PO Box 220
Davilla TX 76523
info@kallistogaiapress.org
(254) 654-7205

Cover photo:s: UK Daily Mail & Adobe Stock
Poet's Photo: Argyle and Monroe Photography by Jenn Harrison
Cover Design: Tony Burnett

ISBN: 978-1-952224-38-6

Distributed by Ingram Lightning Source

Library of Congress control info available on request.

HUNGER HOUSE

POEMS

JESSICA TURCAT

CONTENTS

Il pleut des voix de femmes comme si elles étaient mortes même dans le souvenir...

Guillaume Apollinaire "Il Pleut"

SOME WOMEN

"It was night, and the rain fell; and, falling, it was rain, but, having fallen
it was blood."

  —Edgar Allan Poe

Some women suffer, catch their breath, go on breathing.
Some women labor only a hollow gourd, then stop
Breathing. Some women rise from the stained mattress,
Leave the house behind, walk shiftless until their soles
Blister. Some women pilgrim to *sanctuaires à répit,* rest
Their rotting corpses on shrines under a medieval sun.
Some women wait for a bead of urine, an eyelash flutter,
The skin's fade from waxen blue to white. Some women break
Storm clouds, let the rain cry the length of the panes.
A plague on that house and that house. Why not this house?
Some women bury their secrets beneath a blanket of river,
Watch the baptismal waters churn. Some women swallow
Their tongues, taste the blood twinge with that irrevocable bite.

SKYWALK

I read of a woman who trod a tightrope, once
blindfolded over the frothing Niagara gorge,
another time her ankles and wrists manacled.
After each performance she told her story
to shaking heads. Reporters only asked
the obvious questions and misquoted her
in newspapers until interest inevitably waned.
From the front bow of my stone cottage
I would not have seen the quarter inch wire
stretching the length of Rainbow Bridge,
only her silhouette, a slight blemish inching across
the crescent milieu of Horseshoe Falls flooding
her faculty until she set each chained foot down
in another country. How she must have worked
later that day to wring out her sodden skirt,
draping lacy undergarments, each a white flag
fluttering on the line, to bleach in the sun, a new
awareness of the ground swelling beneath.

EXPOSÉ

You are a trick of a girl posed against a mustang, the soft white of your legs
burning on the hood. A man plops his tongue in your mouth, says *You will be beautiful*

when you grow up. Now smile for the cameras. When the picture develops
you are smiling on the burgundy shell. Your mother says you are so beautiful

you will be dangerous. When you grow up your mother will teach you to hide
each flaw, to limit your time spent outside, to limit your time spent indoors.

To hide your crazy, to push it away like a trick of a girl, you will learn
to limit your time spent on everything. When you grow up men will say

you are beautiful, and you will believe every lie. Now smile
for the cameras. You are beautiful. When you grow up you won't be

like your mother. You will learn to please a man with your mouth
in more ways than one. You will be dangerous. When the picture develops

you will grow crazy, hiding each flaw. Now smile for the cameras.
You are beautiful. Your closet's ordered like a bookshelf. Read the gowns

from left to right to get the whole story. The breast cups collapse, wait
to be filled, for men to say you are beautiful. Your mother will teach you

to wait to be filled. Read the gowns right to left to make yourself sad. You are
beautiful and sad. When you grow up your legs won't burn. You won't wait.

ON MY WAY TO HEAVEN
— Stockton, Missouri 2005

Itinerants on the shore have taken off their shirts this morning
to reveal the raw glow their flesh holds. The deck hands shout
in an ancient cadence, release a reefed sheet, and hoist it aloft.
I watch their rituals with religious devotion. One man, shoulders
broad as the flag above, stands near the mizzen, blacks out the sun.
Both boots planted on polished planks, he rocks back, cups hands
across brow, spits—I think how he could bend two ropes around
my bed frame, trade this heart for a terracotta pot, then steal away.
I watch him climb atop the sailboat's mast. He sways above me,
lifts his hands toward the sun, and falls back with complete faith
that the harness around his waist will hold. Below, I am laid out flat
on a freshly-scrubbed deck. My skin as white as those new sails
taking their first breath after the winter months. The wind catches,
and I watch the top half of his body swing back and forth freely
against the May sky. *You're going to die,* I yell with a nervous laugh.
He pauses. Ospreys circle the ripples for a shadow darting beneath
the surface. The sailors pour another round on the dock. The boat
rocks. I finally relax, spend the afternoon thinking of an answer
after he yells back down to me: *Can you imagine a more beautiful way?*

A GATHERING OF MANNA

5

a soft rime on spring's bitten flesh
she appears like manna with the morning dew

the weight settles across his lifelines

heavy as heaven in the hands
hands that offer flat cakes
cakes that turn to honey on the tongue
the tongue that whispers mine, mine, mine

already she knows

he will soon tire of the taste

INSTINCT

A house wren rests on the white sleeve of a sycamore not unlike this house-
wife amid her morning ritual. Except this place is no longer my home and here
I am no wife. In the passing dawns, through the drifting brume, we regard each
other as if across a kitchen table. She's perched atop the floral painted nest box
I nailed to the fence-post. Last summer, following the second breeding, she left
that hole; this spring she staked claim to the front porch railing. After a rainstorm
subsided I poured a glass of Bordeaux, watched as she pecked a tree swallow
to near death a few feet from my wicker chair. The defeated bird flapped forward,
one wing pitched slightly higher than the other, paused a moment before she caught
her harmony. Cerulean feathers flitted in her wake: across the yard to the shelter
of trees, then beyond the tree line, woodland, deep enough to swallow any shadow.
I knew she was the same wren, returned. Some say leaving is a lifelong process.
No point asking why a woman stays. Head tilted, she studies me as if to confirm:
*We are Midwestern by choice. We have black walnuts in our blood. We have moss-
laced rocks beneath our soles.* For one moment we align as equals, every creature:
rooted, winged, broken, unconscious, clawing. Perhaps it has always been
this way, except we worry about the daily trifles of putting on and taking
off and stitching holes we accumulate in the process. The wren soon shifts
her attention back to the stalks of peppermint invading the front beds,
appreciating how victory dies in the face of hunger. I've lived long enough
to recognize when we must question what we see: when everything we thought
had been questioned by those who built the binary systems dissipates
like last night's fog. Then one morning seven speckled orbs rest in her roost.
In Scripture, seven—the symbol of completeness, perfection. Seven sacred
feasts of Israel. She's added spider egg sacs, meshed cottony cocoons mid tangled
coarse twigs with grass, feathers, pine needles. She leaves only to feed, drops
curls of cabbage moth caterpillars to six gulfs until they want more than she can
suffer. I move to her corner of the porch; she dives at my head, circles
a wide parameter, dives again. I devour her shrill melody. Admire the grit.
Her familiar hope to hitch this intruder's attention with sharp wind-borne trills.
When she fails to sate their desire, one by one they forsake her. How insignificant
my possessions compared with what she teaches: How to starve. How to lure
death away with archaic song. How to take flight, without permission.
I do not think she will return. Alone, I watch a myriad of spiderlings
swarm her abandoned home, consume the final—faultless—bedded shell.

CRACKED COUNTRY

"I am not a monster." – Omaima Nelson
"I ordained that nothing should be more feared than an oath."
    —aretalogy hymn by the goddess Isis, Cyme inscription, 2nd Century C.E.

something hatched inside the first time

no stranger to knives, burden of female
flesh beneath the blade, cut-glass
cheekbones, chastity, locked knees
against the cracked broadside
of rawboned anger, riven skin un-
raveling down the back, a little weak

trickle until the country springs to green
on green on green, except, not green—red
battle bruised, smack of lips

                it's so sweet

to touch, to taste—we are all flawed
imitations of Isis. do you still listen
to our prayers? could you, once more,
gather the hewn limbs, order all things well?

tell me what I want to hear, *sweetheart—*

something hatched inside, woke hungry

ALONE WITH HER REFLECTION

"If Edward and I meet in the Great Hereafter, he will know that I loved him, and that I only left him because my conscience would not let me choose the world and have any peace."
—*From* Tirzah Miller's Intimate Memoir, *October 30, 1875*

We did not say our prayers that night.
       We met on the balcony of the main parlor
            and entered one of the solemn private rooms.

A single bed defined the closing interval
       between us. I looked at the warping hardwood,
            unlaced each boot, pulled off the day's stockings.

Only inches away, he hovered, a selfish sin
       I'd yet to stop, and I could barely see
            his contours, as if he had already left me

and this was just his specter coming back
       to tell me he was leaving with conviction
            this time and I should not search for him.

Once I heard the Committee assigned him
       to come to me again, I took the morning train
            to Joppa to listen for answers to questions

I'd never asked myself. The cottage matured,
       immersed in seasonal respite. Heavy-lidded
            eyebrow windows slept behind knotty pine.

Nothing moved; too early for the ice
       fishermen huddled at Fish Creek's mouth
            to hoist up their small huts. The rainclouds

had yet to accompany autumn; a cluster of leaves
       colored a belt around a wooden boat knuckled-
            under on the shore. Limbs forgotten beneath

Oneida Lake broke the water's horizon further out
       than I had ever ventured. Two pieces of driftwood
            dimpled the façade: *Soul they had not,*

sense they had not —How much remains submerged?
>Then a crane, pitched on one wing, dipped down,
>>skimmed the shoreline before descending squarely

on the surface. The wings' breadth numinous,
>hallowed. I could not focus the moment it took
>>to land, and had I not seen of the hidden bole

I might have thought it angelically perched
>on the water's veneer that shifted green
>>to yellow to murky white under a grey sky.

When I imagine leaving this earthly paradise
>for the world's, it is not without fleshly desires.
>>We could live out our days together. I'd scatter

corn to the chickens out front while he split
>kindling for the winter, letting the curved universe
>>stretch before us like a garden edged with prairie

grass so high we cannot see beyond the next bend.
>At dawn rediscover the figure we held the night before
>>and the night before that. I could let my hair grow

over my shoulders until the ends touch each nipple
>when I undress for him, become fully aware
>>of my anonymity among the skirts sweeping

the city sidewalks. I know the type. Their intrigued husbands
>tote them along on weekends to peek into our existence
>>while cloddishly roving the grounds of the Great House.

The pedestrians look at each other differently,
>as if admiring Lady's-slippers rather than the inspired
>>image of one of their natural born brothers or sisters.

They are always polite, though, mashing each crumb
>of strawberry shortcake between the silver-plated
>>prongs of their fork. A memento of their exodus

from societal standards. I couldn't trust them
          anymore than the flit of beauty that reposed
                    as a slip of black plume with red crown blazing

across the spinney. From the bank I couldn't see
          the fowl with its beady eyes, but I wanted it gone.
                    I grabbed a rock, stripped from the knees down,

waded the embankment until the mire gave.
          I hurled the rock. It skipped and skipped,
                    skipped and then was gone. Still nothing.

My undergarment molded to my thighs,
          and when I sloshed back to the shore
                    I couldn't feel the tips of my toes.

I waited for hours to hear what I needed
          to hear, and still I was not certain until
                    he was with me. His fingers touching just

the arch of my foot. So intense that I felt the urge
          to kick him from the room and yet I wanted also
                    to gather his words together, backstitch them

with silk thread into the folds of my trousers
          until they fused as one smooth stone on which
                    I rub all regret, because we do not exist outside

this moment in this room, this mansion.
          We are tethered to the language of the leaves
                    soughed by winds that rip the white tides,

the faint cry in the rusted chains of the porch swing,
          the conversations between red-crowned crane
                    and water's bruised surface— these whispers

I know as certainly as his vows, and I know
          the edifice of sacrifice is not without challenge.
                    I know the natural always submits to the spiritual,

and I know we will never see each other again. I know
          all this as surely as I know we never outgrow the tailoring
                    of our childhood religion; we never outrun our demon.

MOUNT ZION, WINONA, MISSOURI

I'm pleased with the earthworm that survived
last night's downpour and now writhes along
the broad leaf of a defeated sycamore. The sun
breaks, sets the orange leaves ablaze against

wrought iron fencing that pierces the horizon.
Perhaps I could be buried here after all, maybe after
I'm reduced to a few cups, I could trust someone
to toss my ashes among the plastic flowers, faded

cuds of color, that line the concrete markers
of my ancestry. The wind rustles the silk petals
around every headstone, except one whose name
I still refuse to mutter. I can't bring myself to leave

flowers on the grave of a pedophile
who got away with it— even if he is family.

THE WID'DER WOMAN

"Their houses look with scarlet eyes
Upon a world of sin;
And every man cries 'Whoa, alas!'
And every man goes in."
                —"Sisters of the Cross of Shame" ballad by Dana Burnet, 1888

Rumor had it she was a husband killer,
turned homewrecker. I'd see her front porch
sitting at sundown, a dull bulb diffusing
the night with its yellow dartle. Her hands:
lace curtains quivering before an open oriel,
and when those bare feet brought her to town,
mama'd spit on the sidewalk the way she taught me
not to, said, *All things can be bought, son, sure*
as all things have a price.

Every bullet needs a target.

Ammunition was cheap and mama knew
the ways a woman could relieve her heart
with guns. Gave her something to do with the weight
of her own hands. She'd wrench me awake some nights,
then tote through the backwoods, burnt oil fields,
drop a sack of bullets down in red dirt ruts
that once led to a salt pond. She took the kick
back to back to back. Not until the bald sun welted
our bare shoulders at high noon would she quit
shooting her bolt-action needle on the Texas
-Pacific railroad running away from the cracked
country foundation of our weatherboard house
that collapsed only to remain a ruin in the hill's recess
among shells of houses stacked like defaced boxcars.

Every wife knew the widd'er woman.

Even now, I can draw a bead alongside the buried vales
and depressions written among those twin slab tracks,
forever lost in the chickweed's scalloped edges.

Mama, when we goin' home this time?
Mama, ain't you tired?

GOD, CHILD

Propped up on a greasy barstool, I display
the length of my legs as a few glance
at the entanglement of steel and flesh,
lotioned and glossy flesh under tinted lights.

I am eleven again, laid out flat in the bathtub,
toes hinged on the faucet with a can of Colgate
and a pink razor. In long confident strides

I scrape the lather off, curve around my ankles,
up the tightened muscles to the rough skin
stretched over my knees. With razor posed,

my mother's voice interrupts from the other
side of the plastic shower curtain: *Good girls
have no need to shave above their knees.*

I sit there rubbing my new legs back and forth
under water topped with soap and tiny hairs
and wonder why. A decade later I realize

my mother must have set in another bar,
in another town but with these same legs
crisscrossing and toying with those same men.

I have had years to watch my mother closely.
Listen to her talk of trucks backed into woods,
when she'd had one too many Fat Tires, fat lips.

I imagine if she were here she would smile
and shake her head at me, shake her head
then profess—*God, Child. I have been there.*

DOMESTIC TRINITY

    I am the woman who creates
the whirlpool's core by stirring and stirring, steam
rising from crocks of carnal potpourri, mulled
to the skeleton. A snip of lavender, pinch of parsley
for good measure. My hands fall asleep
wrapped around the thick paddle. They dream
of teacups, honey rims.

     I am the woman who baptizes
every berry in a bowl of chilled water, patting each
dry with her swatch of white linen. I'm the one
butternutting the tranquil curves of the fall squash
to a muculent pulp. The Lazy Susans whirl
carelessly as I polish the silver: fork, knife, spoon—
fork knife spoon— forkknifespoon.

     I am the woman who blesses,
sanctifies the corner baseboards with my cloth,
burnishing scars smooth, laying hands on the tired
doorframes, window sills that offer the clearing
clouds up for redemption. I propel the waters down
stream. Despite the living labor of each day, the Lord
always rives the faithful home.

BABUSHKA DOLLS

Barely able to stand, she cooks the family breakfast.
Scrapes the butter from the wax paper. Wipes the butter
from the knife onto the edge of the iron skillet.
Then folds the wrapper, corner to corner,
and files it in the back of a drawer.

Sometimes all you have is the butter on the wrapper.

She turns back to the stove. The butter
slides down the side of the skillet, sizzles away.

I've never heard her say those words.
Only heard you, father, tell your seventh-male-child-version
of grandmother's lessons of poverty, of lack, of depression.

I remember a painting in her dining room.
You remember too. Frame still hanging on the same nail,
on the same wall, since we were both children
old enough to blush over the voluptuous bathing women
but still too young to understand their curves, their power.

Does she know I want it when she dies? That I pray
her death is as peaceful as her Sunday morning ritual?

The family eats breakfast on the floral couches,
the cushions stained from years of this tradition.
She talks about the preacher on channel five:
After this man is another man.
Then a black and white western.
It's always black and white on Sundays.

I slip from the conversation, pass the painting
of those waiting women, and creak down the stairs
into the basement where I read for hours from her novels,
paperbacks with the beautiful front cover lovers,
yellow and creased. The words so seductive
page after page. She had a cousin, I've never liked,

build special-sized plywood shelves to hold them all.
Spines line one full wall round the corner
to the middle of the far side where they stop
at an old bed piled with empty shoe boxes, dusty
plastic figurines. Babushka dolls she collected
when grandfather was stationed overseas.
His clothes still hang on rods around the room.
His uniforms stand at attention. Beside them,
his daily clothes slouch on their hangers.
Neutral styles from a harder life, too dated
for the cousins to steal. Rough overalls. Scratchy,
square-cut jeans. A pair of old boots, still muddy.
Would he even wear them if he finally returned home
after his long battle? What would he say to his widow
sitting in her recliner watching the gospel channel?
Would he laugh: *Woman, why you kept all this crap
so many years? *Twenty-five? No, closer to thirty now?

Your mother doesn't wear her wedding band anymore.
When I suggest we should have the ring re-sized
because it's too small for her finger, my mother,
who prattles around aimlessly trying to fit herself,
shakes her head. *No, she's not been able to go down there
for many years now.* Her voice catches and drifts back
towards the basement where I gather the painted dolls,
crack each woman like an egg, and dig the identical,
smaller version out of its dark home. No arms to reach
out for the other, I line them up. Each a stair step
ending in the baby lathed from a single piece of wood.

Father, I have known pleasure, known her missing
double-buckled platforms, but I cannot picture
my grandmother as any doll but the matryona
who holds everyone safe inside her. I don't know
how she came to own a fresco of twenty naked women
lounging in the goddess bathhouse. Tell me
how she felt crossing back over the Pacific
alone, the liquid earth heaving and sighing.
Did she breathe the salty air? Store it deep inside,
deciding she would never leave her house again?
Father, did she ever rise in the middle of the night
to stare at those majestic women, and then
walk through her consecrated home, naked,
bathed in moonlight, floating through the remains?

DOLLHOUSE

"I thought how unpleasant it is to be locked out; and I thought how it is worse, perhaps, to be locked in."
        - Virginia Woolf

Already you're playing house, rearranging the furniture in your mind.
        Lift the roof, reveal
the grid of rooms, the long hallway, the long table centered in the dining room
        off the kitchen.

Who is the doll when the dishes need clearing? Who is the mouth
        to smile while serving
the cherry pie on the windowsill? Look out the window,
        past the floral embroidery curtains,

to the blank wall of another room in another house. Yours is a house
        within a house.
The window, only a mirror cleaved to the wall, reflecting the house
        within a house onto itself.

The mirror is invisible without its reflection. Stand in front of the mirror.
        Your mother tried
to hide this from you: your reflection is only an imitation of another
        doll playing house

somewhere in another reflected house. You should not learn
        the secrets of your mother
until you have learned to hide your own. The dolls, still
        positioned at the long table, wait

for you to return. You cannot explain to the other dolls how
        the house has swallowed them,
how they are only reflections of something greater diffused into chairs,
        how their appetites

are not their own. The dolls search for you. Where is a doll to hide in
        a house with no windows,
only mirrors reflecting what is hidden? How does a doll pretend
        to eat sweetened cherries,

knowing she is already swallowed whole? How does a doll continue to smile,
        knowing
that if she refuses to play, any moment the roof can be torn away,
        the interior exposed?

COUNTRY CREAM
— Clever, Missouri, September 2007

She clutches the paddle, positions the base
between her legs, russet-caking across the kneecaps.

I was once like you.

Her shoulders, broad as oxen, tighten as she pushes
the paddle deeper through the thick liquid, pulls
our novel friendship out of the hazy curl of smoke
that drifts from the cigarette dangling on her cracked lips.

I inhale the smoke, take it as deep inside as I can,
watch the white of her knuckles turn whiter.
Believe me, she continues, *that road*—she pounds
the bottom of the tub, huffs—*always ends poorly.*

Thin bubbles churn to the top and burst.

* * *

She taps the lip of the beer bottle again.

Flies disappear, fade into twilight, quiet
enough to hear the wind shift a row or two as it breaks
through twenty-two acres of sweet corn fields.
In a few weeks they'll be plowed to stubble.

We had a mountain lion, few summers back.

I say nothing, stare at the stalks, full from the early rain,
turning to reflect a slight glow from the harvest orb.

I saw her too, right here from this stool.
Thought it was a dog at first—until she moved.
Feline. Unmistakable.

She skims off a layer of fat.
Pours the dregs back into the wooden tub. Silt unravels
like thick yarn piling between us.

Word travels out here, sure as seasons.

The men tried, each morning leaving with rifles in hand,

but never found that trophy.

* * *

I'm deep in marriage now, she confesses.

We leave the cream to sour overnight
under the porch's constellation of cobwebs.

When my husband walks out to the front fields,
drops to his knees, and prays for enough
from the crops for our family to get by on —

I remember why I married him.

This life's hardest when I walk barefoot across the yard,
offer him a slice of chapple pie and ask him to take me,
trembling, like a teenager between the stalks. Forgive me.

Help me remember why we wanted a family and a farm
when everyone else in the world seems content
with merely driving on past our whitewashed fences.

She rests the smooth spat across the top of the barrel,
looks back at me, to what cannot be said aloud,
and the lies that divorce the distance between us.

Harder still when he says nothing, refuses
to climb off the idling tractor.

* * *

The night loosens around us. With our undershirts damp
from the day's sweat and an empty bottle half full of butts,
we pretend to listen to the panting earth, and find ourselves

19

hummed back to present tense by the field's nocturnal pulse.

Still, I mutter, *we could if you want.*

The last of the blackberries glisten through their tangled vines.

Trust me, she says before she stands, drops the last smoke
into the bottle — *such curiosities never last.*

The screen door slaps shut behind her.

Our words circle like the rusted blades of the fan.

        * * *

I tug off my gumboots, stuff the socks down the necks,
feel first the step's worn boards, then damp grass
between my toes. I could run for miles and never reach
another porch light. This kind of expanse compels
the odd connection:

A kitten suckling the sow's teat.
The extreme dance of warm air spiraling upward,
only to be undercut by a swift cold wind.
The farmer's leg raked into the combine.

The moon slides behind a shadow
and each shadow gives way
to another shadow.

The house and the barn, even the silos
have disappeared.

I close my eyes, sense something
stir behind the stalks that arch over my head,
something hungry, untamed,
something that managed to slip from her own death.

THE CAVITY

A woman with no history is so much more intriguing than
A woman with no heart. In fact, she's the only reason why

You came to the party. And even though she looks striking
In her fashion that's not even fashion yet, you soon realize

She can't hold her liquor and all of her stories are fiction.
Then the woman with no heart is in front of you and says

She'll let you put your entire fist in the hole where her heart
Once was and she raises her fist, smiling with childish wonder,

Like her science teacher just explained this magical equation.
You make a slightly larger fist, raise it to hers. You both smile.

Except when she takes her shirt off you can see the cavity
And all its blackness — you had imagined that it might pulse

Red — and for the first time you think to ask her how she lost
Her heart and so early in the game. Then you remember

The woman with no history and realize that you missed your
Chance because now you're just someone she's already met.

TEOTWAWKI

Once that brutal, thick fist of Siberian cold rages down
a starved throat, the blood slows quickly. Fingers spread
throughout the body, freeze each vein and meaty organ.
When SHTF, no one tolerates delicacy. Forget that weak,
pussycat-eared, tutus-prancing for a pretty picture nonsense.
Witnessed babies in Yemen gnaw their fingers to gory stubs
trying to turn bone into tit. Nature evolves harder or dies.
When men can't eat, they'll use any warm hole to discharge.
No argument. No question. No confusion. One fragile heart
beat dimming inside a breaking cage. Watched a Muslim
woman birth in a mud hut. Sow that she was: left the newborn,
ate the placenta raw. Only one identity marker matters –
famished. Grappling to survive, Bosnia, '93, dropped MREs
disappeared like snowflakes on an IFV. A child could be had
for a tin can of *tushonka*. Hospitals became slaughterhouses.
First month, city dwellers hacked down every tree, burned
doors, window frames, floorboards. Their blackouts not even
a footnote in local textbooks now. As a translator, I'm adept
at pinpointing what is not repeated in mainstream narratives
as well as homing in on histories bound to repeat themselves.
I can be as gray as any man. Nothing sexed about me except
the fact that I can use every part of a bird, down to boiling
chicken feet into gelatinous curried treats. I plan to survive.
I stockpile ammo. 90% of gen pop will die after an EMP attack.
I'll glock any zombie steps foot on my property. Total darkness.
Muscle memory. Newbies don't think about the black market
value of condoms. As the medical industrial complex collapses,
those plastic discs turn into gold medallions. Boredom spreads
faster than syphilis. I have tubs of antibiotics, tiny bottles
of alcohol, matchboxes, and cigarette packs for bartering.
We are in the fourth turning. World War III already started.
Pope whatever-the-fuck-his-name-is envisioned omens
of greater destruction and desolation. I don't need fear porn
or to believe in a divine prophesy to see that a new world
order is emerging. Global elites digging 35 mil dollar bunkers

seven stories below sea level. Not a matter of if, but when
that Dooms Day Clock strikes midnight and man's inhumanity
towards man mushrooms on multiple horizons. Too late by then.
I'm not talking about toilet paper wars. Try crafting a sarcophagus
strong enough to stop radioactive contamination. Chernobyl
cleanup won't be completed until 2065. Get past the polar bears,
the Svalbard Seed Vault operates 20 m into a sandstone mountain.
That arctic archipelago was built to withstand a direct asteroid hit,
but not even one of the 2.25 billion seeds sealed in three-ply foil
packages will ever land in the hands of scum like us. Let me be clear.
Rice is a tropical plant. One kg requires 4,000 liters of water
and fertile riverine alluvial soil to create a heavy, clay, loam texture
rich in potash and lime. A simple lima bean or dried kidney bean
grows for 110 days before harvest. Three months to die without food.
Three days without water. Less when operating in a calorie deficit.
Translation: One is none. Two is one. No fifteen-minute city
grocery stores or gas stations. What you got stocked is all you got.
Get your houses in order. Stack your pantries. Rice and beans.
Stack your closets and bathtubs. Stack every room to the rafters.
Take inventory. Look your children in the eyes. Then keep stacking.

OCCIDENTAL PANTOUM

-After the young influencer posed in her orange gown against the burning sky, September 2020

All children cut their teeth and crawl away.
I worry how many babies are being born now.
[*deep breaths*] The planet's literally in crisis.
I'm depressed, too *ennui* to get out of bed.
I worry how many babies are being born now.
I try to describe my problems with hashtags.
I'm depressed, too *ennui* to get out of bed.
No point praying. The protests are exhausting.
I can't describe my problems with hashtags,
So I tweak my profiles religiously for more likes.
No point praying. The protests are exhausting.
My therapist altered my medications again,
So I tweak my profiles religiously for more likes.
I truly care about the heartbreaking forest fires.
My therapist altered my medications again.
I'm supposed to write my thoughts and impulses.
I truly care about the heartbreaking forest fires,
The starving children, and I crave chocolate ganache.
I'm supposed to write my thoughts and impulses.
Meditation never helps. I'm obsessed with saving
The starving children, and I crave chocolate ganache
But I can't find a *patisserie* within walking distance.
Meditation never helps. I'm obsessed with saving
Every message from my followers. I've worked hard,
But I can't find a *patisserie* within walking distance.
I've considered moving. I've even catalogued
Every message from my followers. I've worked hard.
It's art: a social critique of contemporary culture.

I've considered moving. I've even catalogued
Beautiful pictures online. I have to find the best place.
It's art: a social critique of contemporary culture.
I want to make a difference. At night I scrutinize
Beautiful pictures online. I have to find the best place
For my next shoot. I promise my intentions are pure.
I want to make a difference. At night I scrutinize
Photos, perfect my filter on the glowing horizon
For my next shoot. I promise my intentions are pure.
My plan is simple: keep calm and keep taking
Photos, perfect my filter on the glowing horizon.
My parents say, "Nothing's wrong; this will pass."
My plan is simple: keep calm and keep taking
Deep breaths. The planet's literally in crisis.
My parents say, "Nothing's wrong. This will pass.
All children cut their teeth and crawl away."

THE TILLAGE
for the woman scalped by her panther

Ask me again about the jaw clench— clean
  through a severed deer leg and the quiet
languor that accompanies the pacing shadow
  after feeding time. I'll tell you of the emptiness
   that comes with any passion— the pitiful
  ache of loving that which only obeys hunger.

The first time she reached for me, my heart
  lunged back in its cable mesh, stupendously
alive, aware only of the crude blood
  coursing through my veins. The betrayal
   so subtle: a frail graze across the boot tips
  lipped on the berm, as if we touched by chance.

I backskuttled. The wide mouth
  bucket tipped over, rolled into the hollow
feeding range. She didn't pounce as I imagined
  she might wild, across the fallowed continents
   toward the taut throat of a jackal. She froze,
  focused. Scurried forward, dragged the carcass

back to her perch. Flatfooted, paws spread wide
  open, she hunched over the hulk, head tilted close,
began the rhythmic rock with auric eyes
  closed. Muscle and bone, the nightly victuals dropped
   into the sawdust mounding the cage corners,
  blown confetti after a spring formal.

The next time was different; she waited for me
  to turn away first. Rules are always broken.
I knew the stainless steel wire would give
  against the weight. Don't ask questions
   when you know the answer. The challenge
  is to negotiate the confines of our captivity.

Would it surprise you if I told you
		I wanted in? I wanted to touch the fulgor of black
rosettes against the black pelage. Please— Nothing
			more than the rapt mewl and sinew stench, the hopeless
					situation of being wrenched under the rend
			separating our two worlds, ethereal as vibrissae.

Please— She's slinking across the Kalahari desert.
			All teeth and tongue. I'm her red hartebeest, exposed
thoughts licked pure. Please— Let me go
			where natural grace, ancient as the puce dirt breach
					between us, winnows the pain. Not until sun's swell
			does she continue her fence line vigilance.

You wouldn't understand. A woman like me
			needs the security that something waits for her,
needs to stare into the vulgar pulp and come back
					with an answer. A woman like me knows better,
						lies down anyway, plays prey for the shameless
			hunt, gives her unsanctified flesh wholly to desire.

ORO BELLE SALOON, ARIZONA, 1904

for the dove who lingers upstairs, Christian name forgotten

Pocked moon went milky blue.
Wick is spent. Oil long dry.

Come closer. I'll strike flint to tinder.

No one to hear except the mule
And the ghosts and me, but if your fingers
Feel the cold keys, the piano's tune
Strikes without deference to our dark.

        The dead don't dance.
Some sit outside the window, tap
Their feet out of rhythm. Others shake
You from your drunken stupor. As habit,
I wake each morning, still
In this body, forsaken
Same as the wagon trails that hairpin these hills.

Follow me. Stair creak reminds you
You're alive.

        The dead don't shiver
On nights like ours. The harrows
Of the damned freeze the veins gold.

A Confederate soldier left me
This gunboat quilt. You can trace
The *broderie perse*, appreciate
The skills of desperate women.

I imagine you
Came to inspect what was left

Untouched.

          The dead don't covet
Gilt like the breathing. I promise you
Know nothing of fear.
                    Fear pulses.

            Fear veins, lightening

Flowers on rock face. Fear waves
Of thunder. Fear hungers. Fear desires, appetites
Left unbridled.

            The dead don't worship.

My god, refined by fire, you shall be

My fatted calf. At your cloven feet, I will
Feast. I will spin and flit beneath
The horns of your headdress.

                  Fear fires.

Fear flames

That tongue the shimmer from your skin—

            The dust to which we return.

MOTHER UNDER BLANKET HOLDING DECEASED DAUGHTER

a memento mori

I.
Hold every muscle
   still. Do not breathe.
Do not even think
   about breathing.

        You are absent,
         an apparition. Nothing
        more. Quail beneath
          grief's aphotic veil:

static as a guardian
   at the gate,
silent as an angel
   at the grave.

II.
Shhhhh, listen—the sea turns
      a menagerie of wingless mortals
         beyond the seething sand and yet

this ancient circle weaves us
      all into its loom, and the brevity
         of life is but that of a wave crashing

against the shore. Child, tis only
      the moon that drags the tide back
         toward the ocean's belly. I would

carry you once more, but already
      you slip from my fingers, the burden
         of this pallor too much for me to bear.

III.
Take comfort—
        the absurdities of birth
fly from us when death descends,
        drapes around the stiff
shoulders like a prayer
        shawl. I did not ask for this
gift. Now I know the ache
        behind the clipped blossom.
Mother, if possible, I would
        smile for your pleasure.

My aunt asks if I want the death plank.
The thick board, leans against the back
wall of the smokehouse, long enough
to hold "a human body as it was carried
from the home through the second door,
the one that remains locked, of course,
because of the spirits." "The spirits,"
I repeat, nodding my head, "of course."
She uses the passive voice *was carried*
as one might say *her heart was carried*
on her sleeve or *her heart was carried*
between his teeth. No one in the family
has used that slab for three generations.
Everyone who might remember customs
such as how to prepare dead loved ones
on the kitchen table, has died, and they
forgot to tell the family why we should
hold on to an artifact that once held so
many of us. I tell her I could repurpose
the black walnut wood into a distressed
coffee table. I imagine my house guests,
their intrigue, and the vogue dinner party
conversations about its history. She stops
as if paralyzed, the way a mourner might
linger, dumbfounded in the warm interior
before falling in line with the corpse road
procession. I persist, "Think of the stories
it could narrate." Bridging the diametric
planes of past and present, she tilts slightly
back, whispers, "What about the spirits?"

PRAY ME AWAY
Mother Leeds, 1735

Half the world hunts   the other half. I learned   long ago   to trust
a forest   ecstasy of rot   layered in understory.   Trees walk
you into the barren   stomach of pines   woods close behind.
A woman   can haunt such a dwelling   learn the body   lay bare
an embassy   waiting in umbrage.   I could teach you   to knead
dirt into bread   milk bitter bark   stretch   hide in winter's canopy.
Each branch   asks a question   feels for answers.   Each leaf
archives a myth   rustles stories   to the silk cocoons of the gypsy
moth   until they split   open in mid-   summer heat.   Legends
inked in black   arched patterns on their perilous wings.   Listen
the natural world   unlocks at night. Curse   of the callow. Fear-
scented. Guttural   body scream.   Death closes   swiftly. Vulnerable
must keep watch.   Never trust   eyes that cannot see through dark.
You maneuver as if   the body will never   betray you   stray
unwary   movements   creature that has never   run so far   it left
body behind   felt spirit   splinter from thews   wrenching
pain   caught   breath.   Then you discover   strength.   Mothers
know this trap   tight as birth canal   womb's   taut mouth
crowning the new head.   What happens after you spawn   undying
cry   a baker's dozen? Labor-heaved energy   expelled   now
unfolding now   moaning   converting before you are able to lay
hands on   flesh.   How naïve you are   to think you can resist
the unwanted   animal   will the devil   back from your bed   fawn
your eyelashes   wake   untouched   overwhelming hunger   vanished.
Stop thinking you   understand   what I'm telling you   stop trying
to unriddle me   you haven't listened   I already warned you   I am
the ambassador   I control this virgin   territory   you can't unearth me.
you can't blink   me back. You can't you can't you can't   pray me away.

SKY LANTERNS

Wild children bound across a cut wheat field
with painted bamboo cages to light candles, release
a hundred ballooned flames for the October horizon.
The oiled rice papers expand, slowly ascend
over the rows of upturned faces. She imagines
each luminescence—an eviscerated soul
floating like jellyfish from a bleached coral
to the water's surface. Her thoughts drift along
the hilltops with them. By dusk they will crash
against a telephone pole or a building's window
in the nearest city. The hoi-polloi shuffling over
the remains as they hurry along to a luncheon.
Maybe one will make it to the border, settle briefly
on a stream's alluvial sediment before it succumbs.

BABY JANDOLYN

I.

They left this town after the accident.
My truck met their bull chewing its cud.
When I didn't see Ed weaving the wire
back in place I headed over. The heifers
suffered most. Stood spraddle-legged,
balking in their stalls when I arrived,
udders engorged to veiny white globes.
Heard them even before I turned down
the dirt drive. Three days gone I figured.
Must have stolen out in the dead of the night.
Up and left. Probably couldn't handle
the town's talk. The way I see it, though,
at some point, all fifteen year olds fuck up.

II.

We couldn't stay after the accident.
Finding the baby that way got to Bobby.
The mineral-rich water preserved the body;
coroner said the bruised wales on her neck
matched the final story her mother told.
It doesn't seem natural what that girl did.
Mothers, even young ones, don't do that.
They don't let their babies slip through holes.
Mothers don't let their babies float for days
in some well while the family's searching
all hours, hollering over the hills and praying.
Mothers pray. Mothers protect their children.
We had to leave that town, never look back.

III.

Been around the dead on this job, but that
changes you. Wife turns off the lights—I see
that bundle materialize from the void.
Until I can see even the wet hairs on her
limp arms. Took over an hour to pull her up.
Everyone just standing around, staring,
waiting for something. I expected her to cry
when I flipped back the swaddling blanket,
blue giraffes dancing with pink hippos.
Fear will make a person do crazy things.
That mom didn't think, merely reacted.
Saw her baby dangling and panicked.
Plucked her up and tore off through the woods.

IV.

Twisted dandelions. Jandolyn laughs
when I pop their heads off and the buds fly
across the blanket spread under the oak.
She rocks back in her swing. Leans forward.
A phone rings in the house. She rocks back.
From the window I see the infant swing.
She laughs. Throws her body forward and laughs.
I lick the milk from my wrist and heat the bottle.

              The screen door slaps shut.
I see her from the porch, from the front steps.
I see her from the edge of the blanket.

V.

Truth is I was going to marry Jules.
I bought her an ice cream cone and she cried.
Never took a lick; let the cream run down
her arm and drip off her elbow. I watched
as ants crawled around the mess, turned white.
She was stunning and tragic all at once.
I told her we could leave, that I'd take care
of her—and the baby—she kept crying.
I swear I would have stolen my dad's truck
and took off. We'd sing country songs.
She'd prop her feet on the dash, fall asleep.
We'd drive away until the eddy,
a rivulet, turned into an ocean.

TUKANUKARU

I never said you were the owl nor the mouse wrangled
beneath bore of talons, only that I thought of you
    when their shadows skimmed the Alamogordo desert.
        Split rock blossoms and rose clusters spread at my soles
            as if to further remind hitchhikers—*you do not belong here.*
       After several days holed up in the Blue Swallow, I tired
of soaking in the clawfoot tub. I hadn't planned on staying
away but the thought of returning to you became less
    pressing with each passing hour. Once the sky dusked,
       I took to the street if only to feel the pavement pant.
          Mammillaria cluttered ditch lines along the Mother Road.
       I was staring at a buffalo skull wedged on a fence post
    when this Bronco tore down Boulevard in a dust cloud.
Back plate read Pottawattamie, but there was nothing
    native about the homegrown country boy hanging out
       the window. He turned his radio down, hacked and spit
         a brown glob onto the sidewalk, then offered me a chew.
       Seeing as I had no one else offering me anything,
    I took a wad and asked for a ride. A woman can't survive
out here without collecting a few tricks. I climbed in,
    straddled a case of beer, torn open, and took a swig
       after he drove a cold Modelo between my thighs.
         Wasn't long before we were at the motel. Once he shut
       the door on the glowing pink and green neons saturating
    the parking lot I warned him: *Some women don't fight clean.*
He smirked, planted a shit-caked boot firmly between me
    and the bed, then tugged the chenille spread to the floor
       with one jerk. I could tell he was new to being in control.
        So when he finally asked my name, I said Pocahontas.
       And when he asked if Pocahontas did this sort of thing
    often, I lied again. He sat on the corner of the bed, mattress
bowing down. He was even younger than I thought.
    All cotton-denim and sweat. He exhaled, said he wanted
       to brush my hair. My hair, of course, lambent as ebon
         oil that flows beneath bedrock, untouched for centuries.
       I know women who say you can never tell what a man is
    going to do in the dark. That's never been my experience.
No way was I going to come. Just wanted to see how far
    I could take this skin hunger. See if anything had changed
       since a man last touched me, tasted me. A man who didn't

love me or expect the same in return. He moved differently
enough, didn't tell me his damn life story, didn't care
if I got off or not. Maybe that's what I wanted all along.
Pay-per-night room. Rotodial phone. Bar of soap.
This boy, who probably bags at the local Shop-N-Save
for beer money, moaning beneath me. This simple boy,
who didn't mind the lies because he craved sex and my body
was sufficient. I could enjoy what I had been waiting for.
I could relax, give in, and focus on how hard he was
compared to the soft curves I had taken on. I started to
forget who I was, where I was supposed to be. Except
the body remembers what the mind tries to erase.
In the dull yellow lamp light, white droplets slipped
from my left nipple as I arched my back, then a few more
from my right, leaked onto his chest. He opened his eyes.
Lifted his head. Every muscle in him, in me, tightened
as tiny puddles pooled in the contours of his stomach.
The letdown came seconds later: a long swell driven
by some deep pulse far away. I ached. The heaviness
made me punchy. As I sank onto the clammy sheets
he moved on top, battened me down with both legs.
His mouth enveloped one fevered nipple, then the other.
I couldn't breathe. I wrapped my hands around his neck,
felt his tendons flex and flex and flex. He didn't stop,
like he had just discovered life and death inhumed
in the same rootbed of an overrun garden, one he'd been barred
access to for so long that he forgot such a place even existed.
My mouth was dry as the riverbeds when I woke;
sun burned the edges of the curtains. The boy had left
nothing except a few crumpled bills on the sink,
flattened beneath my hair brush. I raked the contents
of the countertop into my bag. I wanted to leave
New Mexico, wanted to make my way to El Paso
where the canyon floor's licked clean and cliffs bite
back against clouds that constantly swallow sky,
where the mind's smothered because there's nothing
to feel except the constant breakage of stones
at my boot tip, and there's only the unrelenting
screech of a dying mouse overhead to wrench
a mother's heart in two. Sometimes the mouse escapes; sometimes
the owl savors the game more when it resists, lets the mouse think
it can escape — but no matter how many ravishingly
devastated landscapes I hunt down, I can't stop myself
from scurrying back to you. No — you're neither
owl, nor mouse. You're the desert, blood-bright,
awash in sunlight, endless country of paltry and pain,
the hardscape that exists whether I want it to or not.

WOMAN COMMITTING SEPPUKU

"Live briefly but gloriously, One's evanescent life is but a preparation for death. The fall of the blossom is as moving as its beauty on the limb and the final moment, as ceremonialized in the ritual of seppuku, is indeed the moment of truth."
— *Jack Seward's* Hara-Kiri: Japanese Ritual Suicide, *1968*

woman is designed for death

       did you expect a virgin's
           silk handkerchief
       perhaps my signature
           finger-scratched in carmine

you would not be so apt to let

     another's blood
            if each moon
     your own slipped
       dark and healthy
       between the thighs

     an eager offering on moss
              -laced rock

woman learns young

     to control
     pain   to bind
     her body   to embody
       her bind

       and when necessary
          escape

her internal battle yields

         tender prey

    the womb

can swallow its own flesh
cud its share
spit out the remains

how easy
            then the blade

let me show you how

        respect is gained
                    for a man

he has only to carve out
the wound he forgot

            I bleed white

camellias until white
camellias blossom white

        camellias

            death is never earned

ROAD WASHED OUT

Even with chevrons signaling us left, we knew

we could brave the brief stretch   through wet
meadows recently cleared for deer. A boldness
bred only in country childhoods. We slowed
in the depression of the third   hill, allowing
the hood lights to narrow   on the divorce.
We watched water cull   knuckled roots, cleave
rock and detritus. The earth below   betrayed,
dregs swiftly passing through the hollow,

                                        the breadth
wider   than our arms could reach.
                        How could we keep moving

                                                forward?
Strange   to recall how long   we paced the edge,
        the way we both studied   the scar

silently   in awe   of our false certainty.

HUNGER HOUSE

I returned home,
started eating. The brass door handles
                scraped the roof of my mouth
        until I bled, but the silk curtains slid the length of my throat, so smooth
                I thought of angels combing swollen rivers after a spring storm.
        When I finished
I wanted more. I flipped broken fan blades
                in each cheek, contemplated
        what came next. The muscles lacing my tongue buckled while molding
                oriental rugs into tight globes. I watched myself as I ate mirrors.
        I ate the face
of the wall clock, felt its hands spinning in my stomach.
                I ate until time stopped,
        then I ate some more. I went for the antique furniture, gorged the dark cherry
                wood desk topped with stained glass lamp. Then, the semi-sweet
        over-stuffed leather sofa
and matching recliners, spicy throw pillows.
                Then, bite after bite,
        wedding photos gone. I tasted the couple's terror. Then, microwave, blender,
                toaster, bistro table, rococo china buffet—no time
        to order appetites
onto such thin mantles! I slurped the bathtub
                in one gulp, chased it
        with towel rack, shower curtain, bath mat, medicine cabinet, and popped
                each light bulb on the vanity mirror like caviar. I shoved
        thick dresser drawers
down my throat, one after the other, paused
                to lick my raw lips, then dived
        head first into the delectable California king. Funny thing about memory
                foam, each mouthful tastes better than the last. Sensory cells,
        a spun carousel:
cheetah after giraffe after deer in mid-
                leap after unicorn—head reared,
        mouth agape, plastic silver mane blown back to expose crazed eyes
                and before I could savor another morsel I hit the innerspring

coils, kept grinding till
there was nothing left but the rubbled
                        brim of the box frame around me.
        Exhausted, I chewed my way out. Why stop when there was so much
                crown molding, plantation shutters, polished herringbone floors?
        I must admit,
I hesitated before the voluptuous refrigerator.
                        Its burnished skin beckoned. I had to
        have it all. I fed on humming heart, gnawed sinewy wires,
                licked grime-packed years off square tiles, still cool to touch.
        Hunger pangs
wrenched: *Feed me. Feed me.*
                        I crawled on all fours. My brutal hands
        rimmed closets, clawed for orts. I panted. The house trembled. I had only to cut
                our throat when somewhere inside me, deep in the masticated ruin,
        a faint ringing
echoed in the stripped silence: someone worried
        if I arrived home safe and sound.

CONSUMPTION

"Never eat more than you can lift." – Miss Piggy
"In death . . . they have become apparitions."
– "Wave of Violence Swallows More Women in Juarez,"
New York Times, June 23, 2012

I.   The routine: rows
Upon rows, women bent
Over the endless
Conveyor belts, churning
Spools strung like stars
To the florescent-striped heaven.
Hook after hook, the needle
Pierces the worked
Cloth faster than a finger can
Move from beneath it.

You soon forget
The mouth under your white filter,
The disposable masks.
The boss-men
Check for menstruation
Each month, stamp their own
Proof of purchase:
A swift right-handed
Blow to the gut. If you're
Lucky they deliver
Their verdict at the end
Of your shift, daybreak.
The Mexican sun
Flowers blossom, tiny fists
Punching through dirt packed
Hard as pavement.
I cradle my stomach on the bus
Ride home, past the spread
Legs of Juarez's La Equis.

II.   Miss Piggy squeaks *hello*.
I've sewn her ears
Crooked
A thousand times.
Miss Piggy wants to eat
Me for dinner.
Her newly-stuffed fingers unclasp
The thousand silver buttons
I fastened that hour.
Her toy platoon breaks
The assembly line, rips
Tulle shirts from their identical frames.
In unison, they pull fingertip
After fingertip: purple satin gloves
Slip to the floor,
Pile to the ceiling.

Miss Piggy wants me
Buried alive.
She throws her wigs across
The plant. A mountain of blonde
Curls tangle in the corner.
Miss Piggy stares at me.
She cannot blink.
She is perfectly priced.
Miss Piggy squeals *goodbye*.
Good / buy
Echoes a thousand times
Across the American border.
Miss Piggy is plush and pink,
Beautiful
Naked bodies
Heaped on this single soul.

III.   You who knew a thousand deaths
        As no reason for silence
        Visit me at night: *Ni una mas.*
        Ni una mas. Ni una mas.—
        Dare me to follow you
        Downtown, dance to the forced
        Rhymes of dead female
        Poets in our red lace
        Dresses and monochrome
        Sugar skulls.

        You etch a spider
        Web across my powdered brow.
        Black petals bloom from my irises.
        You sew my mouth shut, a black cross
        Stitch penned down my lips.
        I thought we were playing
        A game. Why no
        Mirrors in this fun house?
        You pinch me.
        I don't wake, I can't
        Scream. I pinch you,
        You disappear.

        I am alone in this dream.
        What good is poetry?—
        When the Chihuahuan desert dry
        Heaves women's torsos, the blue
        Factory-issued smocks still double
        Knotted around their lean hips.
        What good?—When gone
        Their nipples, gone
        Their tongues, their eyes, gone
        Their bare feet, their hands
        That only last week whip
        Stitched ivory leather
        Totes with royalin leather piping.
        What good?—*Ni una mas.*—
        Wake. Wake. Wake.
        The machines must be fed.

RUDBECKIA IN THE ATTIC, 1933

for the farmer's wife found swinging

If only this heat would break—obliging
as a yearling nestled into her first bridle.
Seems like whole world's got the fever.
Stagnant air's hotter than expected—sickly
sweet, peppered. Dries the throat.

I miss my old broodmare.

Only this netted mass as company now.
My fingers dimple the moldy foreshank.
Already turned. Only brined cuts left.
Carcass sways—rope rubs wire
strung from crossbeam. They hold.

Let me serve us tea and cake on bone china
with a hand-painted golden flower border.
Then, we'll ride through the back fields; see
how they grow crazy along the fence line.

Now for the basic two-point: weight
on the balls, lift slightly, lean forward.

Gently now—like a lady.

Once evening light strains between rafters,
plate missing, he'll find us both cured.

One less mouth.

ACKNOWLEDGEMENTS

The poems in this book have appeared in the following journals and have received the following recognitions:

Aesthetica Creative Writing Anthology: "Exposé" (Finalist in the 2013 International Creative Works Competition); American Literary Review: "Alone with Her Reflection" and "Skywalk"; Aquillrella: "Mother Under Blanket Holding Deceased Daughter" (Honorable Mention in 2013 Poetry Contest); Arts & Letters: "The Tillage" (Finalist in the 2013 Rumi Prize in Poetry Competition); Backbone Press: "Mother Under Blanket Holding Deceased Daughter" (Honorable Mention in the 2013 Lucille Clifton Poetry Prize Competition); Broad River Review: "The Tillage" (Winner of the 2013 Rash Award); Frontier: "The Cavity" (Finalist in the 2019 Industry Prize); Indiana Review: "Pray Me Away"; Kindred: "Domestic Trinity"; Magma Poetry: "Dollhouse" (Second place in the 2013 International Judge's Prize); Moon City Review: "Babushka Dolls," "Baby Jandolyn," "Sky Lanterns," and "On My Way to Heaven"; Off Channel: "The Widd'er Woman" (Winner of the Mississippi Valley National Poetry and Honorable Mention in the 2014 Provincetown Outermost National Poetry Contest); Oklahoma Humanities Magazine: "On My Way to Heaven"; REED Magazine: "Rudbeckia in the Attic, 1933" and "Mount Zion, Winona, Missouri" (Winner of the 2012 Edwin Markham National Poetry Prize); San Diego Poetry Annual: "Tukanukaru" (Second runner up, 2019 Steve Kowit Poetry Prize); Slippery Elm: "Hunger House"; Spillway: "A Gathering of Manna"; Quarterly West: "Some Women," "Instinct," "Oro Belle Saloon, Arizona, 1904," and "Consumption" (Winner of the 2015 Writers@Work Fellowship); Weave: "Cracked Country"

"Some Women" takes its epigraph from the Edgar Allan Poe short story "Silence – A Fable," 1838. The historical information about *sanctuaires à répit* is derived, in part, from Olwen Hufton's *The Prospect Before Her: A History of Women in Western Europe, 1500-1800*. (New York: Vintage Books, 1995).

"Skywalk" is inspired by Maria Spelterini, the only woman to cross the Niagara gorge on a tightrope.

"Alone with Her Reflection": Italicized lines are from Henry Adams Bellows' translation of stanza 17 of the *Poetic Edda* poem *Völuspá*. According to Norse mythology, Ask and Embla (ash and elm), the first two humans, were created from two pieces of driftwood from the World Tree. This creation myth differs from the Christian Genesis account in that after given life, mind, and sensory ability, the gods never intervened with Ask and Embla's free will— they lived according to their own reason.

"Dollhouse" takes its epigraph from chapter one of the extended essay by Virginia Woolf "A Room of One's Own." First published on October 24, 1929, the essay was based on a series of lectures Woolf delivered at Newnham College and Girton College.

"Oro Belle Saloon, Arizona, 1904," as the epigraph suggests, is inspired by the mining town prostitute, remembered only as Leather Belly, who still haunts the upstairs rooms of the saloon where she was murdered. In 1904 the town burned and only the saloon was saved. It was later relocated to Crown King where it remains today.

"Pray Me Away" is inspired by Deborah Leeds, known as "Mother Leeds" who gave birth to her thirteenth child in 1735. As legend has it, the infant changed from a normal baby into a monstrous demon, and the Jersey Devil continues to haunt the Pine Barrens of Southern New Jersey to this day.

"Consumption" is inspired, in part, by the account of Elena as detailed in Norma Iglesias Prieto's *Beautiful Flowers of the Maquiladora: Life Histories of Women Workers in Tijuana* (Austin: University of Texas Press, 2010).